They Made a Difference

Pamela Farmer

ISBN 979-8-89345-381-2 (paperback)
ISBN 979-8-89345-382-9 (digital)

Christian Faith Publishing
832 Park Avenue
Meadville, PA 16335
www.christianfaithpublishing.com

Printed in the United States of America

Actors

Marilyn Monroe

Charlie Chaplin

Mary Pickford

Halle Berry

Sidney Poitier

Hedy Lamarr

Lucille Ball

Juanita Moore

Dorothy Dandridge

James Earl Jones

Morgan Freeman

Authors

Langston Hughes

Alex Haley

Rosa Parks

Morris Dees, Jr.

Dr. Maya Angelou

Toni Morrison

Alice Walker

Dr. Seuss

Helen Keller

Harper Lee

Civil Rights

Rosa Parks

Coretta Scott King

Dr. Martin Luther King Jr.

Thurgood Marshall
United States Supreme Court Justice

Harriet Tubman

Vivian Malone Jones

Lena Horne

Fred Shuttlesworth

Claudette Colvin

Nelson Mandela

James Hood

Paul Robeson

James Meredith

W. E. B. Du Bois

History

Roscoe Brown

Col. Benjamin Davis

Herbert V. Clark

Airman

Nelson Mandela

Frederick Douglass

Garrett Morgan

W. E. B. Du Bois

Robert Smalls

Morris Dees, Jr.

Dr. Ronald E. McNair

Albert Einstein

Madam C. J. Walker

Claudette Colvin

Walt Disney

Mary McLeod Bethune

Amelia Earhart

Dr. Mae Jemison

Congressman John Lewis

Wernher von Braun

Asa Philip Randolph

Abraham Lincoln
16th President

Christa McAuliffe

James Meredith

Franklin D. Roosevelt
32nd President

Eleanor Roosevelt

Andrew Young

Julian Bond

Michelle Obama

Barack Obama
44th President

Bass Reeves

Vivian Malone Jones

George Washington Carver

Booker T. Washington

Martyrs

Medgar Evers

Emmett Till

Vernon Dahmer

Dr. Martin Luther King Jr.

President John F. Kennedy

Sports

Arthur Ashe

Gabby Douglas

Joe DiMaggio

Babe Ruth

Joe Louis

Mickey Mantle

Jesse Owens

Lou Gehrig

LeBron James

Cornelius Johnson

Wilma Rudolph

Willie Mays

Jackie Robinson

Hank Aaron

Music

Wilson Pickett

Lena Horne

W. C. Handy

Paul Robeson

Johnny Cash

Aretha Franklin

B. B. King

Pearl Bailey

Marian Anderson

Dolly Parton

Billie Holiday

James "Count" Basie

Quincy Jones

Bessie Smith

Ella Fitzgerald

Ethel Waters

Smokey Robinson

Duke Ellington

Wynton Marsalis

Robert Johnson

Louis Armstrong

Mahalia Jackson

Nat King Cole

Correspondence

Pam,

Thank you for sharing your time, talent, and artistic ability with the students you serve. Keep up the good work, Pam.

Tamisha

Dear Mrs. Pam,

Thank you for the pictures. I think you are a great drawer. You really do know how to draw. I just wanted to thank you for all you do. You are a great drawer.

Love,
Katehryn

June 26, 2014

Dear Ms. Farmer,

Thank you so much for the wonderful set of drawings. I am so touched by the significance of your gift. I do hope to put them to good use during the years to come.

All best,
Deirdre Cooper Owen

STATE OF ALABAMA

OFFICE OF THE GOVERNOR

ROBERT BENTLEY
GOVERNOR

STATE CAPITOL
MONTGOMERY, ALABAMA 36130

(334) 242-7100
FAX: (334) 242-3282

November 7, 2012

Ms. Pamela Farmer
1918 10th Street Southeast
Decatur, AL 35601-4422

Dear Ms. Farmer:

Thank you for the beautiful drawings of the Scottsboro Boys and of those involved in the case. It is always a pleasure to hear from citizens like you.

It is certainly an honor to serve as Governor of Alabama. This would not be possible without a world-class Cabinet and staff who work diligently for the betterment of our state. I am enjoying my tenure and your thoughtfulness brings additional validation to our efforts.

Thank you again and best wishes in your future endeavors.

Sincerely,

Robert Bentley
Governor

RB/tv/dr

I appreciate you so much.

Thank you so much for sharing your artwork with us. We love caring for you and appreciate your trust in us.

Paul Tabereaux. M.D.

Ms. Farmer,

Thanks for the great prints of Barney and Andy. That was, and still is, one of my favorite shows. Some great life lessons!

Regards,
Michael Tubbs

ASU
DEPARTMENT OF HISTORY
AND POLITICAL SCIENCE

January 27, 2014

Pamela Farmer
1918 10th St. SE
Decatur, Alabama 35601

Dear Ms. Farmer:

The Department of History and Political Science at Alabama State University greatly appreciates the beautiful artwork you donated to the department and the university.

The department will honor your donation in a special exhibit on Monday, February 17, 2014 at noon in GW Trenholm Hall. Titled "African-American Heroes," the event will be a major feature of ASU's observance of Black History Month. The exhibit will also include a reception.

I misplaced your telephone number. Will you contact me at (334-590-1837) or through my Administrative Assistant, Mrs. Kay Brown, at (334-229-5130)?

We look forward to hearing from you as soon as possible.

Dr. Dorothy Autrey, Chair
Black History Month Committee

Morgan County Archives
624 Bank Street N. E.
Decatur, AL 35601

February 23, 2009

Dear Sir or Madam:

I have had the opportunity to work with Pamela Farmer for the last year at the Morgan County Archives. Ms. Farmer serves as an Archivist Aide and, as such, indexes historical data and assists patrons in their historical and familial research. She is pleasant and courteous to staff and patrons alike and extends aid in a swift and professional manner. Although my knowledge of Ms. Farmer exists in the sphere of work, our business relationship has allowed me to adequately experience her many fine attributes. I would recommend her services to any employer or organization.

Respectfully,

Jessica A. Callahan

Jessica Callahan
Morgan County Archives Assistant

SOUTHERN POVERTY LAW CENTER
400 Washington Avenue
Montgomery, Alabama 36104

Morris Dees
Founder and Chief Trial Counsel

November 1, 2012

Ms. Pamela Farmer
1918 10th Street, SE
Decatur, AL 35601

Dear Pamela,

Thank you so much for sending me the sketches. I understand you had a bit of trouble getting them here.

You have one of those rare gifts and I appreciate you sharing with us. I will place them in our library so that our staff can also enjoy them.

Sincerely,

Morris Dees

MD/jb

Thomas R. Bice
State Superintendent of Education

STATE OF ALABAMA
DEPARTMENT OF EDUCATION

April 7, 2014

Mrs. Pamela Farmer
1918 10th Street, South East
Decatur, AL 35611

Dear Mrs. Farmer:

What a delightful surprise to receive your phone call offering to send a set of your prints depicting your drawings of American icons! Your passion to help Alabama educators teach students about individuals who made an impact during the Civil Rights era, entertainers who laid the foundation for those of today, and legendary sports figures through your visual images is both unique and meaningful.

Thank you for sharing your love of drawing with the Alabama State Department of Education. Your thoughtfulness and generosity is deeply appreciated. It is my hope that your drawings will inspire the youth of Alabama to strive for excellence. Your gift can become an instrumental tool as students work to become the leaders and American icons of tomorrow.

Sincerely,

Sara B. Wright

Sara B. Wright
Arts Administrator

SBW: SSM

The Jackie Robinson Foundation

June 22, 2015

Ms. Pamela Farmer
1918 10ᵗʰ Street, SE
Decatur, AL 35601

Dear Ms. Farmer,

Thank you so much for your thoughtful note and the lovely sketch of my husband. We will certainly treasure your prints!

I enjoyed hearing your story recounting the impact the move "42" had on one father, and I am always delighted to hear how our story continues to move and inspire others.

Again, thank you for taking the time to write and to send your prints of Jack.

Best wishes,

Rachel Robinson

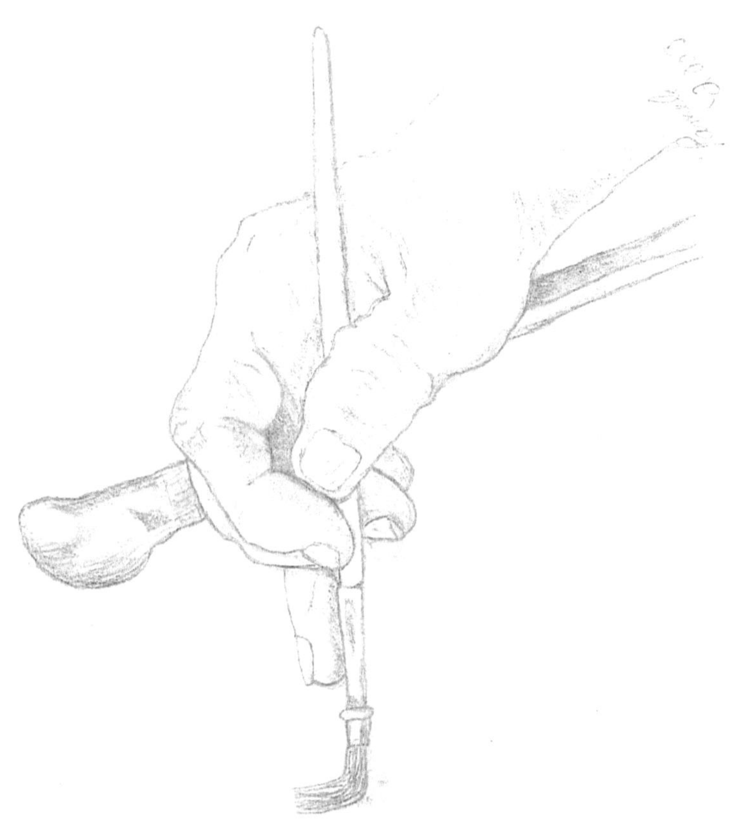

Daddy's Hand

Pamela's Dad, Carlisle Buck Jr.

Pamela's Mom, Esther Murray Buck

Pamela's Son, Michael Farmer

Photo of Pamela, Brother Gary, Sister Pat

Acknowledgments

I am deeply thankful to the people who inspired and helped me along the way. I am grateful to my father, Carlisle Buck Jr., who was my mentor in so many ways, thank you to my brother Gary Buck for your encouragement and to my mother, Esther Murray Buck. She was such a caring force and always looked out for me. To my sister, Patricia Rogers for your love. Thank you to Morgan County Archivist John Allison and to Sheila Washington of the Scottsboro Boys Museum for your patience and assistance as I gathered information and worked on this project. Thank you to Sabrina Smith, Austin High School Library Media Specialist, who was my proofreader when this project went to the publisher and through its stages.

I am so grateful for Decatur City Schools Library Media Specialist Deede Lyons Jones who found photographs as I made sketch drawings of these people who left their impact in so many ways. Last of all, I want to thank Michael Farmer. You are my son and my biggest fan.

About the Author

Pamela Farmer became interested in historical events and people by listening to the conversations of her parents. As a child and teen, she lived in Pensacola, Florida, where she became a beach lover and a graduate of Escambia High School. She worked in the emergency room at Baptist Hospital in Nashville, Tennessee, after high school and then moved to Decatur, Alabama, where her family members have lived since the early 1800s.

She recalls a conversation when she was a young woman with her father concerning the Scottsboro Boys Trial, which occurred in the 1930s. He attended the trial and told her all about the charges, the case, and the trial as she grew up. She plainly remembers him telling her, "Those boys were tried and convicted before they ever set foot in the courthouse."

Her interest in history and current events grew stronger and stronger. As an employee of Decatur City Schools in Alabama, she was assigned to Leon Sheffield Elementary School to take on the role of a "grandmother" to pre-K classes. It gave her great pleasure to get to know the children in the program. She worked with students to improve their basic skills, including reading, and helped the teachers with whatever was needed.

While the pre-K children took their naps, she would go to the school library and draw. The third through fifth graders would watch and ask questions about the people she was drawing. She started the sketches of Black Americans in all walks of life and then incorporated other races as well. She worked as the "grandmother" in the pre-K classes for seven years. Her sketches have been displayed in many places, including Tuskegee University and Alabama State University.